RMS LUSITANIA

RMS LUSITANIA

A HISTORY IN PICTURE POSTCARDS

ERIC SAUDER

TO THE PASSENGERS AND CREW OF RMS *LUSITANIA*

First published 2015
Reprinted 2021

The History Press
97 St George's Place,
Cheltenham, Gloucestershire, GL50 3QB
www.thehistorypress.co.uk

© Eric Sauder, 2015

The right of Eric Sauder to be identified as the Author
of this work has been asserted in accordance with the
Copyright, Designs and Patents Act 1988.

All rights reserved. No part of this book may be reprinted
or reproduced or utilised in any form or by any electronic,
mechanical or other means, now known or hereafter invented,
including photographcopying and recording, or in any information
storage or retrieval system, without the permission in writing
from the Publishers.

British Library Cataloguing in Publication Data.
A catalogue record for this book is available from the British Library.

ISBN 978 0 7509 6280 3

Typesetting and origination by The History Press
Printed by Imak, Turkey

CONTENTS

Acknowledgements   6
Foreword   7

Construction   9
Trials   17
Service   45
Interiors   93
Sinking and Aftermath   101
Propaganda   119

ACKNOWLEDGEMENTS

Thanks to the following for their kind assistance in the production of this book: Brian Hawley, Craig and Shara Anderson, Dan Cherry, Mike Poirier, and Chris and Cindy Sauder.

Thanks also to Amy Rigg, Lauren Newby and the amazing staff at The History Press.

And a final thanks to the many companies that produced the original postcards presented here, all of which capture moments in history that would be lost to us had it not been for their efforts.

All the postcards presented in this volume come from the Eric Sauder Collection.

FOREWORD

Lusitania was an engineering marvel. She and her sister *Mauretania* sparked the public's imagination in a way never seen before. *Mauretania* was blessed with a long, successful career and is fondly remembered today as a ship with a soul. *Lusitania*, on the other hand, although one of the most beloved ships of her day and having set world records for speed and size, ended her career at the bottom of the cold North Atlantic.

The public's interest in *Lusitania* continued even after her loss but for different reasons. She ultimately became a rallying cry for troops on the front lines and propaganda posters, her achievements and successes forgotten.

This volume tells her story, from construction to the aftermath of her sinking, in postcards. Although not an exhaustive history of this extraordinary liner, this book will hopefully pique the interest of some readers to find out more about this magnificent vessel, which held the world's attention but now is known to the public at large as the first victim of total war.

Eric Sauder, 2015

Construction

The earliest-known design for *Lusitania* and *Mauretania* depicted them as three-funnelled liners with an overall length of about 750ft. As the design progressed, it was realised that four funnels would be needed and that both the length and beam of the new greyhounds would have to be increased. As constructed, each ship was a slightly different length because they were built at two different yards. *Lusitania* was built at John Brown & Co. Ltd, in Clydebank, Scotland, while *Mauretania* was built at Swan Hunter & Wigham Richardson, in Newcastle, England. The sisters were the largest vessels in the world until the advent of White Star's *Olympic* in 1911.

This French postcard is one of the earliest known renderings of the Cunard sisters and compares them to the French ship *L'Orénoque*.

After years of work negotiating with the British government, Cunard's chairman, Lord Inverclyde, was able to secure the company's independence for the foreseeable future by obtaining an increase in the yearly mail subsidy and by receiving a low-interest loan to build the two new Cunard giants. Inverclyde was the driving force behind saving Cunard from its precarious financial state and was responsible for setting Cunard on the road to its greatest triumphs of the twentieth century. *Lusitania*'s keel was laid by Lord Inverclyde on 17 August 1904, but unfortunately he did not live to see the ship completed. He passed away on 8 October 1905.

To decide what type of engine should drive the new Cunard greyhounds, an internal 'turbine committee' was formed. Despite what is frequently stated, the Cunarders *Caronia* and *Carmania* were not used as test beds to determine the type of engine – turbine or reciprocating. That honour went to the newly constructed turbine ship *Brighton* and the reciprocating-engined *Arundel*. After a careful review of the performances of *Brighton* and *Arundel*, the turbine committee recommended that turbines be adopted for *Lusitania* and *Mauretania*.

There was also a great deal of discussion among the Cunard board members over what the names of the two new liners should be. As the months went by names were submitted by both the board and the general public, and lists running to several typewritten pages were assembled. After a great deal of debate, the names *Lusitania* and *Mauretania* were chosen on 15 February 1906.

One of the biggest decisions about the launch of *Lusitania* was oddly left until about seven weeks before the scheduled date. Once the matter was given some consideration, it became clear that the obvious choice to christen the greatest liner ever built in the United Kingdom was Princess Louise, a daughter of Queen Victoria. Cunard sent an inquiry to her equerry, but Cunard had left the matter too long. Because of prior commitments, Princess Louise had to decline the invitation.

Cunard then turned to Mary, Lady Inverclyde, widow of the former chairman. Although she was still in mourning for her recently deceased husband, she consented to launch the ship.

This postcard was mailed the day before the launch and was sent to a Mrs Duff in Glasgow. The message reads:

> I have managed to get a ticket for you for tomorrow's ceremony, which is to take place a little after 12. You might try to be down as soon after 11 as you can. I don't know what you will do about George if he wants to come, because there is the strictest orders from the yard officials that no children are to be allowed into the yard at all, & bills to that effect have been posted all over the place. I hope it won't be too great a disappointment, but I thought it best to let you know beforehand.

On an identical card postmarked the day of the launch, the message reads: 'We were seeing the launch. This great boat slipped into the water like a toy. There were thousands of people seeing it. Clydebank was on holiday for the occasion.'

S.S. "LUSITANIA." (TURBINE) LENGTH 780 FEET, BUILT BY JOHN BROWN & CO., LTD., CLYDEBANK.
READY FOR LAUNCHING.

"LUSITANIA," 785 feet long, gross tonage 32,500 tons. Built by Jons Brown & Co., Clydebank. Largest Turbine Steamer in the World. J. McPhate, Clydebank.

For several months before the launch, the area of the Clyde immediately aft of the launch ways had been dredged, as had the River Cart, for the princely sum of £14,141 7s 11d.

On the day of *Lusitania*'s launch, 7 June 1906, the workers at John Brown had been given a holiday to attend the event, and vendors worked their way through the massive crowds that had gathered at the shipyard, selling picture postcards of the liner at various stages of construction. This card is an example of what was for sale that day.

Shortly before 12.30 p.m., Mary, Lady Inverclyde, climbed on to the launch platform, which had been decorated in blue, gold, and crimson bunting. After a few minutes, she pressed a button that released a bottle against the starboard bow and sent the ship on her way.

When the launch trigger was released, there was no movement at first. Then, slowly, some creaking was heard and the ship began her slide into the river, quickly picking up speed. Off to one side, Clydebank Fire Brigade anxiously waited in case their services were needed.

Following the launch, the new liner was towed to the fitting-out basin, where work continued for just over a year to ready her for her place in the history books.

Immediately after the launch, 500 invited guests were ushered into the yard's moulding loft for a special luncheon to commemorate the event. Among the many speeches made were those by Sir Charles MacLaren of John Brown and William Watson, chairman of Cunard. Watson made a special point of thanking John Brown for the fine work they had done and made a special mention of the late Lord Inverclyde and the vast amount of work he had done to save Cunard from financial ruin and bring the company to this, the proudest day in its history.

S.S. "LUSITANIA," (TURBINE) LENGTH 787 FEET, BUILT BY JOHN BROWN & CO., LTD., CLYDEBANK.
THE LAUNCH—LEAVING THE WAYS.
[PENDER,]   [Clydebank.

Opposite: Postmarked 22 June 1907, this postcard reads: 'This is a photo of steamship *Lusitania* nearing completion on the Clyde, one of two largest ships in the world.'

Most of the superstructure is complete, but work continues on the area of the first-class Smoking Room just aft of the fourth funnel. As in any large undertaking, there were numerous delays during *Lusitania*'s fitting out, including a series of strikes. In spite of this, construction of the liner had to be completed on time because stiff monetary penalties would be imposed on the shipyard if *Lusitania* were not ready on schedule.

A HISTORY IN PICTURE POSTCARDS | 15

27 June 1907. After just over a year of fitting out, *Lusitania* left her birthplace for her trip to the open sea. At 11.50 a.m. she departed the yard for her journey down the Clyde, and on her passage downriver she was accompanied by six tugs. Because of her deep draft Cunard and John Brown wanted to make sure that she did not go aground at any point along the way, so for the previous twelve months the upper part of the Clyde had been dredged to an average depth of 34ft at high tide. On her passage down the river, she drew 29½ft. Having completed the journey safely, she arrived at Greenock just under two hours after her departure from the shipyard.

Lusitania's departure from John Brown's yard was dictated by the tides. Because of this, a great deal of work was not completed by the time the ship left for Tail of the Bank. John Brown therefore sent an army of workmen who would stay with the ship throughout her trials to make sure she was ready by the time of her maiden voyage in September.

Thousands of postcards of *Lusitania* were sent in the days following her departure from John Brown. This one was mailed on 8 July 1907. One only wishes that we had the photographs mentioned: 'These are not my taking, but there [sic] good photographs nevertheless!! I've not had mine developed yet.'

Mailed the day after *Lusitania* completed her first two days of sea trials, this message reads: 'July 4, 1907. I thought you would like this photograph of the *Lusitania*, the largest ship afloat taken on the Clyde.'

Opposite: Lusitania underwent much more extensive trials than the vast majority of merchant ships because she was built with government money and any mechanical failure would have been catastrophic not only for Cunard but for John Brown as well. If the liner did not reach and maintain her required contract speed the Admiralty would cut Cunard's yearly subsidy, and Cunard, in turn, would impose a one-time financial penalty on John Brown:

> In the event of it not being demonstrated during actual service during the first twelve months after delivery, that this ship is capable, on a draught not exceeding 33 feet 2½ inches, of maintaining a minimum average ocean speed of at least 24½ knots per hour in moderate weather, the Builders shall pay to the Cunard Company as liquidated damages the following sums …

The penalties John Brown could pay amounted to £10,000 for every tenth of a knot under the contractual speed of 24½ knots, with a maximum fine of £100,000.

3563B   **CUNARD S.S. LUSITANIA,**   ROTARY PHOTO. E.C.
33,000 TONS, 70,000 H.P., LENGTH 790 FT., BREADTH 88 FT, DEPTH 60 FT.

After some last-minute preparatory work, *Lusitania*'s first set of 'secret' progressive trials was held over the course of two days, starting on 2 July 1907. The overriding issue, which became immediately apparent, was the severe vibration in the liner's stern. Within a few short days of the end of these sea trials, John Brown sent a memo to Cunard explaining in great detail each change that they suggested making to the ship immediately. Most of this work centred on the second-class superstructure and consisted of much-needed stiffening to try to reduce the 'rattle' of the stern at high speeds.

Work on the alterations proceeded without delay and, once this was completed, *Lusitania* sailed for Liverpool on 15 July, arriving the following day. Meetings were held on board the liner between John Brown engineers and Cunard's naval architects while she was anchored in the Mersey. Although the vibration had been reduced, it was still not as much improved as had been hoped.

She is seen here on 16 July 1907, shortly after her first arrival in Liverpool, with the Cunard tender *Skirmisher* alongside. *Lusitania* had arrived early and anchored off the landing stage at 7 a.m. That afternoon, assisted by tugs, she was put into Huskisson Dock.

Lusitania was the largest vessel in the world and, as such, caused a sensation when she arrived in her home port for the first time. This and the following few cards record her progress as she is manoeuvred through the locks of the Sandon Half-Tide Dock on her way to the Huskisson Dock. From Huskisson, she would be guided through to the Canada Dock and ultimately into the Canada Graving Dock. *Lusitania*'s beam was around 88ft. The entrances to both the Huskisson and Canada Dock basins were 90ft, leaving almost no room for error.

Still in the Mersey, *Lusitania* is at the entrance to the Sandon Half-Tide Dock on the morning of 16 July.

In mid-March 1904, as the dimensions of the new ships were being determined, a meeting was held with Captain Thomas, the Dock Superintendent of Liverpool; the two senior Liverpool pilots, Messrs Gore and Ledder; and the General Superintendent of Liverpool Docks. A model of the Sandon and Huskisson docks was laid on the table in the boardroom along with a model of a vessel with the dimensions 760ft x 88ft.

Captain Thomas was brought into the room first and gave the opinion that he did not see any difficulty in passing vessels of these dimensions through the 90ft entrance between the Sandon and Huskisson docks. He thought that the arrangement of fenders on either side of the entrance would require special consideration, however. He added that he would not be afraid of the ship hitting the entrance but only of the propellers touching the wall.

When the Liverpool pilots came in and examined the dock model, Mr Gore said that he would prefer taking a vessel of 88ft through the entrance rather than a ship of smaller dimensions, because there was less room for the vessel to 'wobble'.

Lusitania entering Sandon Half-Tide Dock. Although there were three entrances to Sandon, only one was large enough for *Lusitania* to pass through. From here she would move through the dock system to the Huskisson Dock and then to the Canada Dock, where she would stay overnight. The following day, at about 2 p.m., she entered the Canada Graving Dock for the first time.

Having successfully entered the Liverpool dock system, *Lusitania* is tied up in the Huskisson Dock overnight.

Opposite: *Lusitania* entered the Canada Graving Dock for the first time on the afternoon of 17 July to have her hull cleaned and some repair work done to her propellers.

Shortly after *Lusitania* was placed in the graving dock and the emptying of the water began, there was an alarming incident that caused much consternation. As a Cunard memo explains:

> When the water was pumped down to the ship's 25-foot waterline, the after shores commenced to vibrate and crack, and one shore forward of amidships on the Starboard Side jumped out of position. It was thought that part of the launching gear might have adhered to the ship's bottom and displaced some of the bilge or keel blocks, and in order to ensure perfect safety it was decided to refloat the ship and examine the blocks.

The dry dock was refilled with water, and the following morning the liner was taken out so the keel blocks could be examined. Everything was in order, and it was evident that, when *Lusitania* had first been put into the dry dock, the shores had been set up before the ship had time to completely settle on the soft wooden keel blocks.

A view of *Lusitania*'s starboard propellers in the Canada Graving Dock. At some point during her passage down the Clyde from the shipyard or during her trials, her starboard forward propeller had hit something and been damaged. This blade was replaced during the dry-docking.

Left: Sitting high and dry in the Canada Graving Dock, the knife-like bow of *Lusitania* provides an imposing view. The white-painted strip under the forecastle had yet to be changed to black, but that would happen shortly. Note the large crowds that had come out to view the liner.

Opposite: The dry-docking had lasted just over a week, and the process of taking *Lusitania* out of the Canada Graving Dock began at 6 a.m. on 22 July. She then remained in the Huskisson Dock until 26 July. Next to *Lusitania* is *Skirmisher*.

LUSITANIA LEAVING DOCK. W&Co.

A HISTORY IN PICTURE POSTCARDS   41

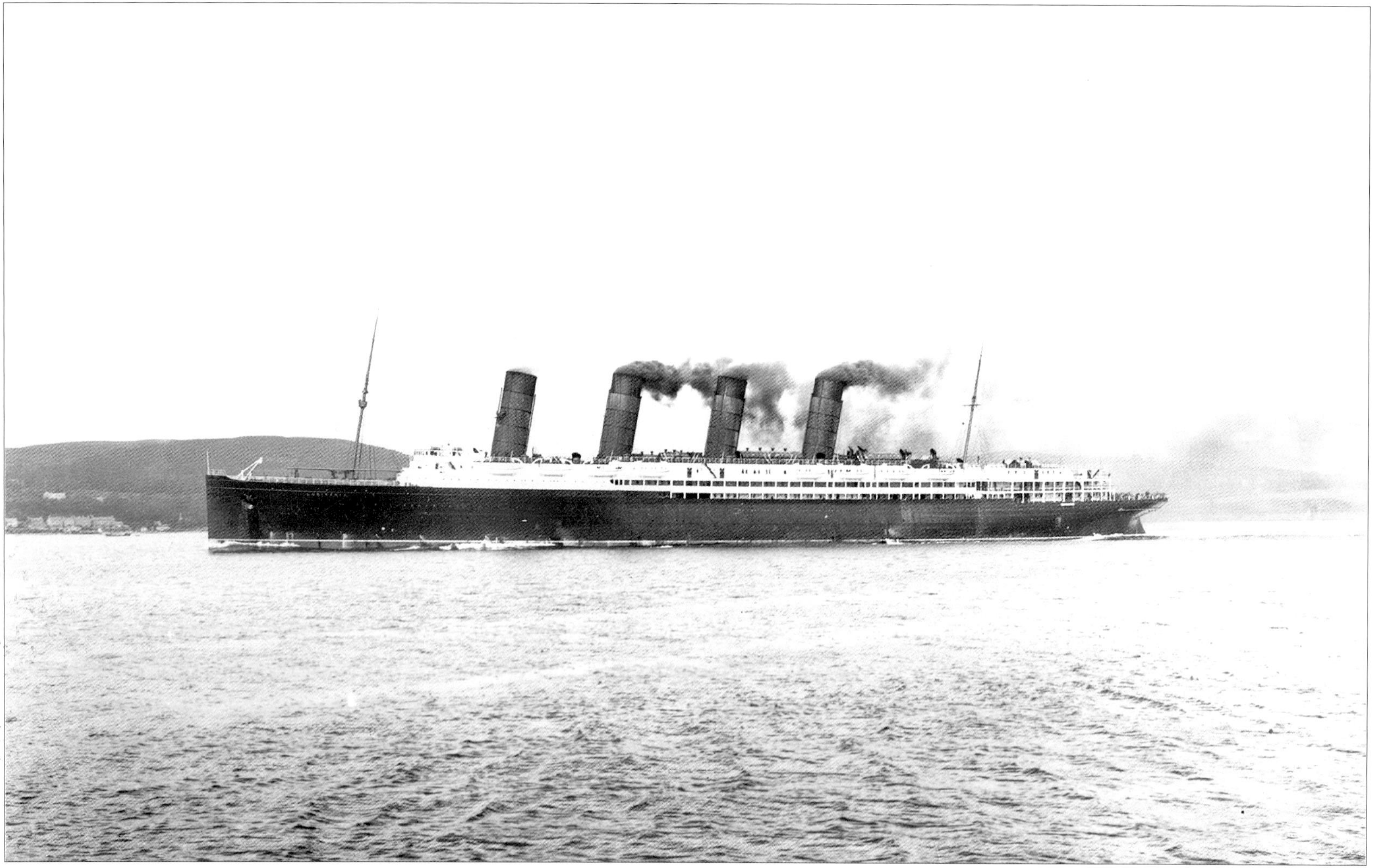

Opposite: Early on the morning of 27 July, another day of trials commenced at 4.40 a.m. Fourteen runs were made over the measured mile at Skelmorlie. The average speed of the first two runs was 25.63 knots. The remaining runs were made at various speeds, ranging from 15¾ to 25 knots.

After these runs were completed, *Lusitania* anchored at Tail of the Bank to await the guests John Brown and Cunard had invited for her trip around Ireland to Liverpool. The companies had originally intended this voyage to start in Liverpool but, because of the unresolved vibration issues and because John Brown wanted to carry out further high-speed tests, the embarkation point was moved to the Clyde.

After the quick jaunt around Ireland, *Lusitania* arrived at the Liverpool Bar Lightship at 9.37 a.m. on 29 July. Her guests disembarked via *Skirmisher*, and at 1.18 p.m. the liner departed once again for the Firth of Clyde to carry out additional speed trials. Despite all the additional work done to arrest the persistent vibration, it was still a concern. The liner was not scheduled to depart on her maiden voyage until 7 September. That gave John Brown and Cunard just over a month to discuss the issue and figure out what was to be done. *Lusitania* returned to John Brown's yard, where even more stiffening was added to the second-class deckhouse.

Just after midnight on 30 July, her 'official' trials began. These consisted of four runs along a 303-mile route between the Corsewall Lighthouse near Loch Ryan in Scotland and Longships Lighthouse near Land's End. Her speeds on the southbound runs came in at only a fraction of a knot different – 26.4 knots for the first run and 26.3 knots for the second. Her northbound runs were made under unfavourable weather conditions, and the speeds reached were 24.3 knots for the first run and 24.6 for the second. Her average speed for all four was 25.4 knots over a 1,200-mile course in Atlantic-like conditions. This was nearly a full knot faster than her contract-required speed, but her trials were not yet complete.

On 1 August, the liner made several shorter runs on a 59-mile track between Corsewall Lighthouse and Chicken Rock. She was then taken on six very short jaunts between Holy Isle and Ailsa Craig. During her official trials, *Lusitania* travelled over 2,000 miles and attained a maximum speed of 26.7 knots. Cunard, John Brown and the Admiralty could not have been more pleased.

John Dunlop, the managing director at John Brown, wrote to Cunard's chairman William Watson on 19 August to let him know that 'on making further inspection of the vessel last week, we find it will be impossible to have everything in order to allow her to leave on Saturday first, and I have therefore decided to arrange for her departure from the Tail of the Bank on Monday night, 26th instant …'. Fortunately for Dunlop, Watson responded that the plans he had made were acceptable to Cunard.

On the morning of 26 August, *Lusitania* departed Tail of the Bank to perform the steering and turning tests required by the Admiralty and then proceeded to Gourock to embark several Cunard directors and left for Liverpool. As she steamed for her home port, her final set of vibration trials were conducted. After the massive amount of stiffening that had been added recently, it was reported to Cunard that '… it was found that there was a marked improvement, and that the vibration, although still perceptible, was not likely to interfere to any appreciable extent with the comfort of the passengers'.

Despite the issues that had plagued the ship since she first put to sea in July, Cunard was obviously happy with the results of the liner's trials, stating:

> The *Lusitania* has just completed the most thorough speed trial which has ever been undertaken by a merchant steamer. Under somewhat stormy and unfavourable conditions she has steamed at full speed for 48 hours between the Lands End & the mouth of the Clyde, making the journey twice in each direction. The total distance covered was 1200 miles, and the average speed of all the runs was well over 25¼ knots.

The following day, 27 August 1907, *Lusitania* was officially handed over to Cunard at 5 p.m. She was now ready to show what she could do.

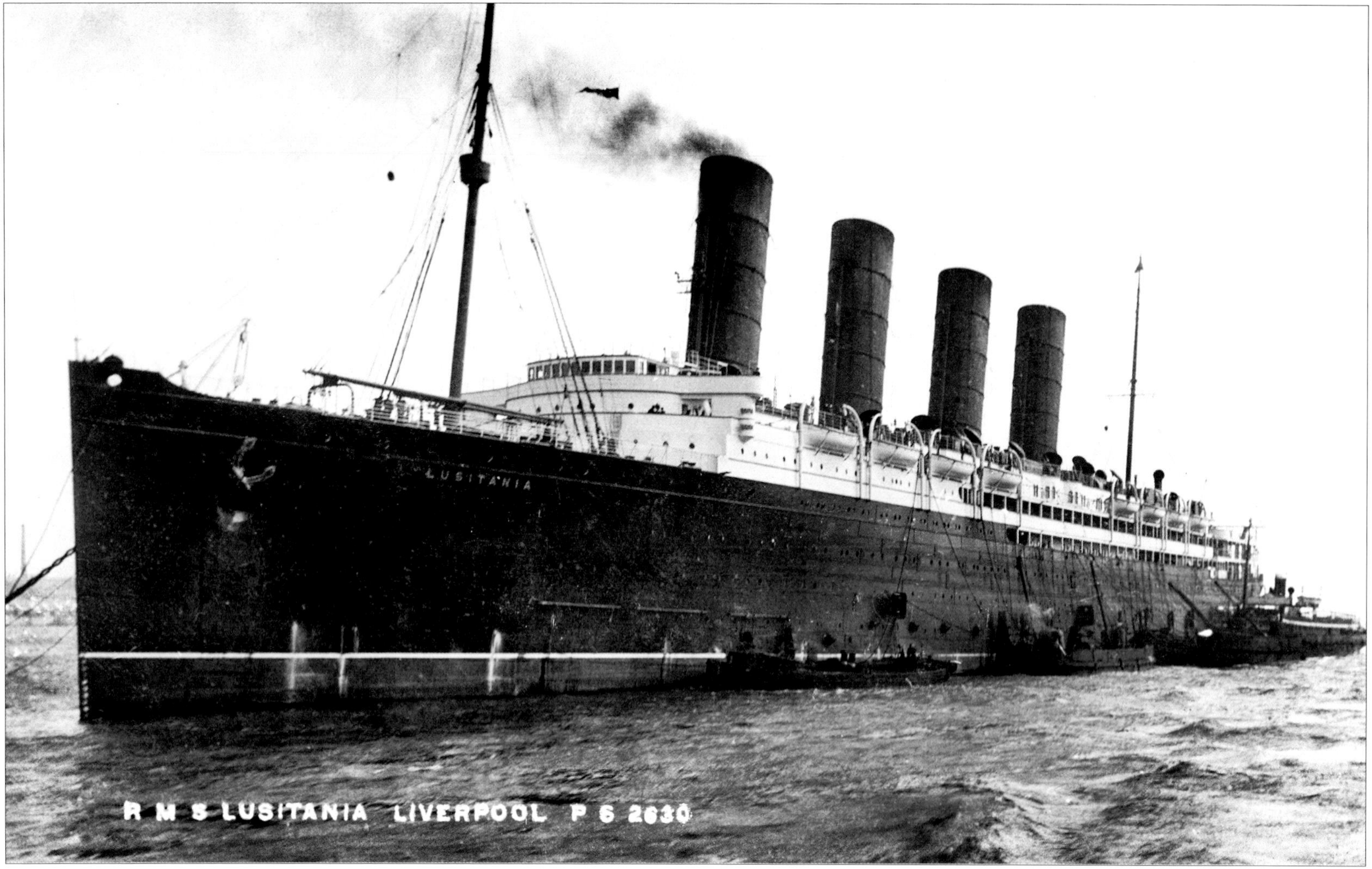
LUSITANIA
R M S LUSITANIA LIVERPOOL P S 2630

Service

Below: As *Lusitania* lay in the Mersey before the maiden voyage, the public was invited to visit the new Cunard greyhound. The liner was opened to the public on 3 September for a fee of 2s 6d. although Cunard shareholders were able to board for free. All the proceeds were given to local charities and at the final count about 10,000 people had visited the liner that day, being shuttled back and forth by *Skirmisher*.

Above: Since 1897 and the advent of the German liner *Kaiser Wilhelm der Grosse*, it was Germany, not Britain, that had truly ruled the Atlantic waves. The German express service to New York far outclassed anything that Cunard or its rival White Star had to offer. By 1901 Cunard was in a serious financial state and in danger of being taken over or simply going out of business.

After years of negotiations, Cunard's chairman, Lord Inverclyde, worked out a deal with the British government to increase Cunard's subsidy and to obtain a low-interest loan for the construction of two new express steamers that would become *Lusitania* and *Mauretania*.

Skirmisher was built by J.&G. Thomson & Co. in Glasgow in 1884 for use as Cunard's Liverpool passenger tender. She had a long and fascinating career. Among her special duties was acting as tender to the Cunarder *Campania* during the Spithead Naval Review for Queen Victoria's Diamond Jubilee and serving as an embarkation ship during the Boer War. When the Cunard liner *Aquitania* was launched in April 1913, *Skirmisher* was sent to the Clyde to assist with the launch.

After sixty-one years of service, she was finally withdrawn in October 1945, with final demolition being completed in March 1947. She was not only the longest-serving Cunarder, but she had carried more passengers than any other Cunarder as well.

From the time she was turned over to Cunard on 27 August until her maiden voyage on 7 September, *Lusitania* lay in the River Mersey tied up to a Cunard buoy in the Sloyne. Last-minute construction work and other preparations were being carried out on board right up to the time she left on her maiden voyage.

Lusitania approaching the Prince's Landing Stage for the first time. Liverpool was her home port for her entire career, but dock space there for large liners was in short supply. To get around the problem, upon arrival in Liverpool, the vessel would come alongside the Prince's Landing Stage to disembark passengers, and once that was complete, the steamer would anchor in the Mersey to prepare for the following voyage. Cunard liners tied up at one of two buoys in the Sloyne called Cunard A and Cunard B.

If a Cunarder came alongside the landing stage any time after 8 p.m., each passenger had a choice of either going ashore upon arrival or remaining on board for an additional night and disembarking after breakfast the following morning. On sailing day, the steamer would be alongside and ready to receive passengers at least two hours before the scheduled sailing time.

50 RMS LUSITANIA

Opposite: One of the greatest boons for the Liverpool Docks in the late 1890s was the opening of the Prince's Landing Stage in 1895. Prior to that time, steamship passengers were required to board any large ship in Liverpool by tender. According to a period newspaper:

> The Liverpool landing stage is the largest and most remarkable structure of its kind in the world. It is 2,063 feet long and 80 feet broad and undoubtedly is the finest marine promenade in existence … It is moored at a distance of about a hundred feet from the dock wall, with which it is connected by a number of covered bridges for foot passengers, and an immense floating bridge, 550 feet long and 35 feet wide, for vehicular traffic. The stage floats up and down with the tide, and it is but little disturbed by the rough gales that frequently make the Mersey a miniature Channel.

Left: Aside from providing transatlantic passengers with a safe and comfortable way of boarding the large steamships, the new landing stage made provisioning the ship a breeze.

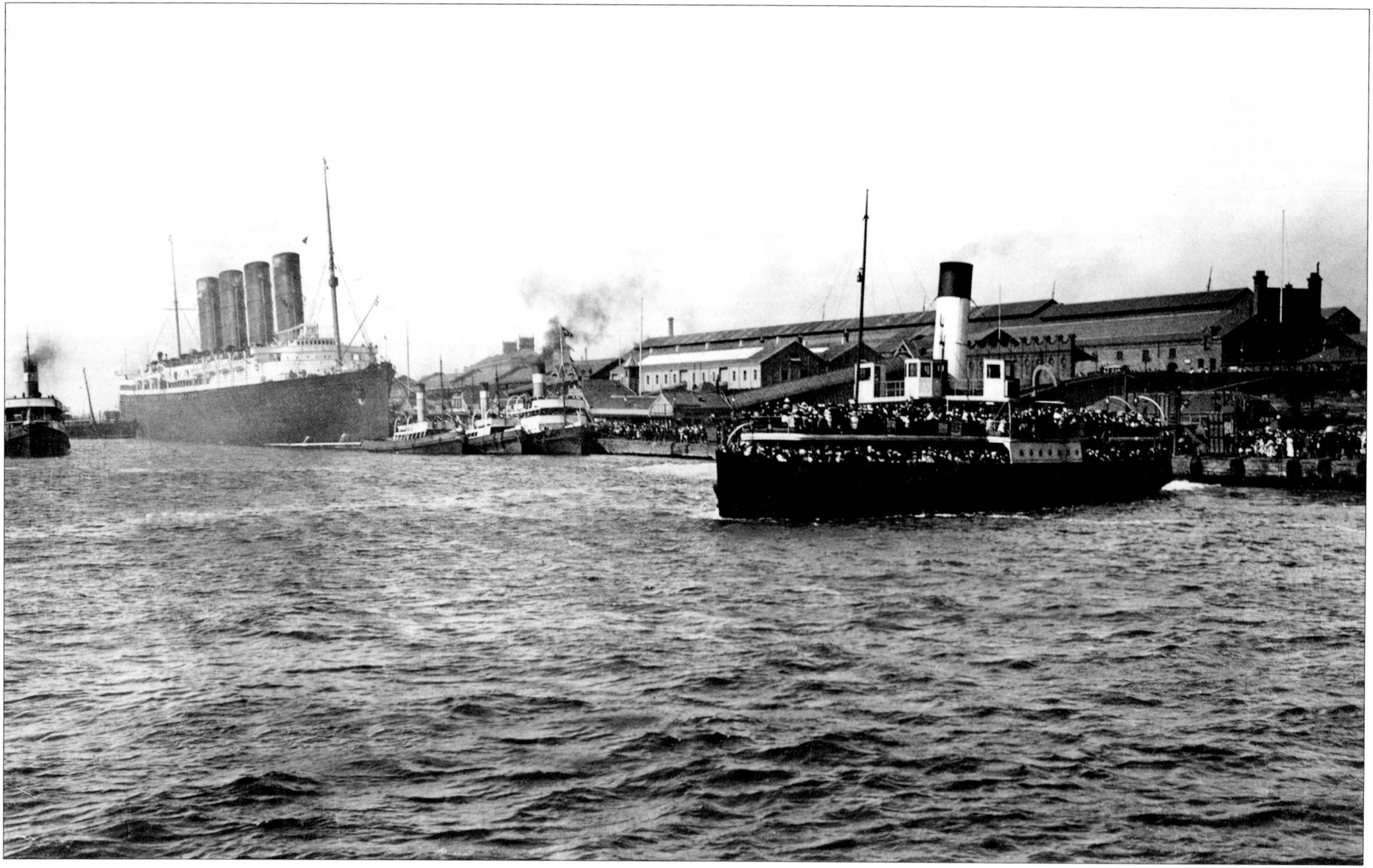

Lusitania lying alongside the landing stage. The Royal Liver Building can be seen under construction to the left. This image dates to the latter half of 1909.

54 RMS LUSITANIA

7 September 1907. The Cunard liner *Lucania* was scheduled to depart the landing stage for New York at 4.30 p.m. Once she had sailed, *Lusitania* would then come alongside and begin her embarkation process. *Lucania* sailed about half an hour late, but once she had cleared the stage *Lusitania* took her place. Passengers made their way on board and began to get their bearings. Although dusk was beginning to fall, the waiting crowds on shore were rewarded for their patience. The new liner was lit up from stem to stern and presented a truly magnificent sight.

Opposite: A busy day at the landing stage as *Lusitania* prepares for a voyage to New York. Anchored in the Mersey, just to the left of the liner's stern, is one of the Cunard 'Pretty Sisters', *Caronia* or *Carmania*.

Two postcards that were taken from on board *Lusitania* that give a good idea of the hustle and bustle of Liverpool on sailing day. The date is Saturday, 23 August 1913, and *Lusitania* had been out of service for nearly eight months while severe damage to her turbines was repaired. The prior December, while making her way through Fishguard Harbour, the liner had to make an emergency turn to avoid a small boat in her path, but the telemotor had jammed and the ship could not be turned. The only way to reverse the liner was to throw her turbines in full astern, which had the devastating effect of shearing off rows of turbine blades. *Lusitania* was not able to return to service until the following August, which is when these images were taken.

A HISTORY IN PICTURE POSTCARDS 57

Finally, at 9.10 p.m. on 7 September 1907, *Lusitania* began dropping her lines and, almost imperceptibly, moved away from the landing stage. The scuttlebutt around Liverpool was of a 'race' between her and *Lucania*. As most people realised, however, that was preposterous. The 14-year-old twin-screw *Lucania* could not possibly have beaten, let alone come close to, the speed of *Lusitania*.

On the day of *Lusitania*'s maiden voyage, one newspaper reported:

> Probably never before has so much interest been displayed in the maiden voyage of a new vessel as was displayed today in the sailing of the *Lusitania*.
>
> As *Lusitania* gathered headway down the river, and every steamer and riverside factory for miles along the Mersey joined in the chorus of goodbys [sic], the din was deafening.
>
> The demonstration reached its climax when the vast multitude broke out with 'Rule Britannia.' This song was taken up by the crowds on the Cheshire side of the river and sung until the ship, with her 3,000 passengers, had passed slowly beyond the sight of the four-mile-long riverside promenade.

The liner faded from view and sailed into the history books.

"Lusitania" passing out of the Mersey.

Opposite: Good weather prevailed for most of the crossing, but for various reasons, including a fog bank one day out of New York which forced Captain Watt to reduce speed for a few hours, *Lusitania* was unable to make a record crossing. She arrived at Sandy Hook at 8.50 a.m. on Friday, 13 September. She had made the crossing in five days and fifty-four minutes at an average speed of 23.01 knots, missing the record by a mere thirty minutes.

952. – Le « Lusitania » le plus grand Paquebot du monde, pénétrant dans le Port de New-York

Longueur totale : 245 m. ; Largeur 26 m. 40 ; Déplacement : 45.000 tonnes ; Puissance totale des machines : 70.000 chevaux Nombre de chaudières : 24 ; Nombre de foyer : 192 ; Surface de grilles : 3954 m. carrés ; Consommation de charbon en 24 h. : 1250 tonnes ; Vitesse à l'heure, en milles de 1852 m. : 25.

J. H.

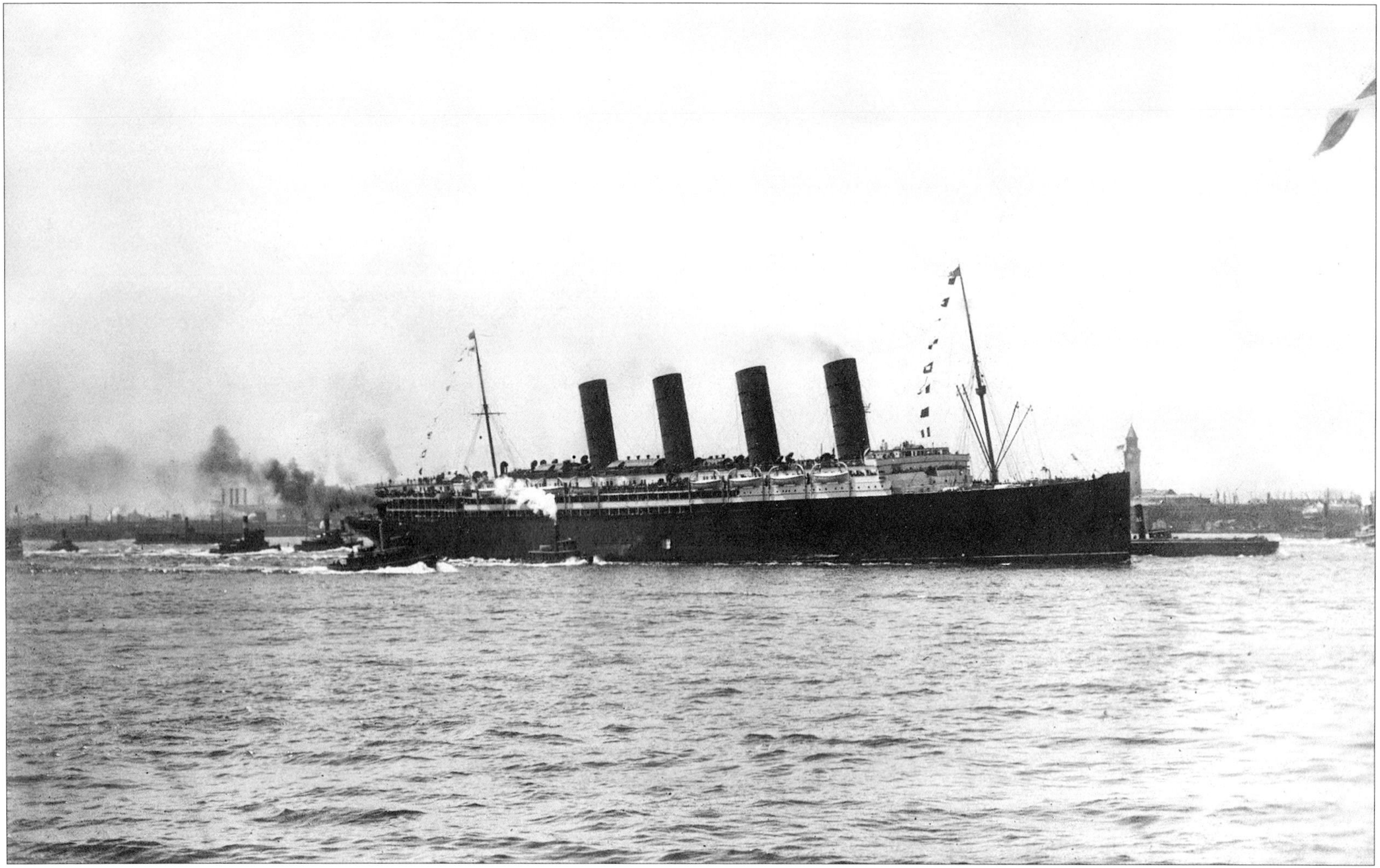

Opposite: After a stop at quarantine so health inspectors could check for disease on board, *Lusitania* made her way up the Hudson River towards Pier 54. Tens of thousands lined the shore to get a look at the new Cunard racer. Flags flew, whistles were blown, and it seemed that everything that could float had come out to greet her.

One thing that put a damper on her arrival was the temperature in New York, which was far above average for that time of year, hovering at around 85 degrees. Newspapers reported that a number of passengers complained about the heat of their staterooms, although it is not clear if this was a general problem on board throughout the voyage or if this was because of the high temperatures in New York.

62 RMS LUSITANIA

These two photographs were taken on 15 September 1907 while the liner was docked at Pier 54 in New York on her first visit. Privately printed postcards were very popular at the time and were an inexpensive way to mail some of your best photographs to friends and family. The crowds that came out to see the ship are evident, and it is interesting to note that the street in front of the Chelsea Piers is still a dirt road.

Despite the enthusiasm shown for the new liner, there were still some worrying newspaper reports about the vibration on board. One passenger on the maiden voyage was Ernest Cunard, grandson of the line's founder and a board member of the company. He took great pains to talk to many crew members about the issue and heard no complaints during the voyage from first-class passengers, even though 'they all came on board primed with the idea that it would be very great'. He did mention that there were still some areas with slight vibration, 'but in [no] case is it sufficient to cause any real inconvenience …'. It appeared that much of the strengthening work that had been done by the builder had alleviated the problem, although it was not completely gone. The final word on the vibration should come from Ernest Cunard: 'Speaking generally, I think we may rest content, that the stiffening which has been added, has taken away most of it, and what little remains must be expected in a ship of such power as this.'

1st and 2nd Cabins of the MAURETANIA and LUSITANIA are ALL furnished with Marshall Ventilated Mattresses

CUNARDER "MAURETANIA"

Any company connected with *Lusitania* and *Mauretania* used their association with Cunard and the new liners to good advantage, and many produced advertising cards to show their close link to the Cunard greyhounds. The Marshall Mattress Company was Cunard's first choice to supply the mattresses for the two new ships. They were to be ordered through Messrs Wylie & Lockhart, one of the firms subcontracting the interiors, but Cunard then discovered that they could save the £200 subcontractor markup by simply ordering the mattresses for *Lusitania* through John Brown, which they did.

One of the more collectible types of card produced for steamships were these, which contained woven silk portraits of the liners. These were produced for dozens of liners in different styles.

WOVEN IN SILK.
R.M.S. LUSITANIA.
Length 790 ft.   Breadth 88 ft.   Depth 60 ft.   Displacement 45,000 tons.

This card is signed by James Birnie Watt, *Lusitania*'s first captain. Watt went to sea as a cabin boy on a sailing vessel and joined Cunard in 1873. Having worked his way up through the ranks, when he was appointed master of *Lusitania* he was earning £900 per year, plus a £100 bonus as commodore if any ship under his command was not involved in an accident.

CUNARDER ARRIVING AT LIVERPOOL

Above: A postcard with a very prophetic message that had far-reaching effects not only for *Lusitania*, her crew, and passengers but for the world as well.

Opposite, far right, top: The first-class Lounge on Boat Deck. A lovely colourised card looking aft. Unfortunately, only a few colour interior cards were ever produced for *Lusitania*; **bottom:** The first-class Smoking Room. When one thinks of British Edwardian liners, one doesn't think that there would have been non-smoking areas. According to a *Lusitania* passenger list: 'Gentlemen are requested not to smoke in the saloons, state rooms, or companion-ways.' The Smoking Room and on deck were the only places where smoking was permitted.

'TIS A FADED PICTURE (4).

A big ship is sailing for the dear old shores,
  And the youth is bound for home;
He longs for one glance of the land he adores,
  As the ship speeds o'er the foam.
Though rich, that old picture he wears next his heart
  Just the same as in days of yore,
Then he vows with that mascot he never will part,
  These fond words recalling once more—

BY ARRANGEMENT WITH MESSRS. FRANCIS, DAY & HUNTER, THE PUBLISHERS OF THE MUSIC.

BAMFORTH (Copyright).

LENGTH 790 FT.   BREADTH 88 FT.   DEPTH (MOULDED) 60 FT.   TONNAGE 33,000.   HORSE POWER 70,000.   SPEED 25 KNOTS.

R.M.S. "LUSITANIA"   THE LOUNGE.   (CUNARD LINE.)

VERANDAH CAFE. LUSITANIA AND MAURETANIA.

Above: As originally designed, the Verandah Café was to be an open-air seating area with a covered overhead but no enclosure on either side. Late in the construction process, Cunard reconsidered this idea and enclosed the room on three sides, leaving the aft end open to the elements. Removable screens were added at a later date.

Under pressure from competing steamship lines, Cunard considered converting this space into a gymnasium that could be shared by first- and second-class passengers. Ultimately, this idea was rejected, and the café received a £580 redecoration, which included wicker furniture, hanging plants, and some trelliswork.

In 1914, a fire occurred here as a result of rats 'eating away the insulation of the wires, thereby allowing contact between two live wires'. The damage was quickly put right.

This card is identical to one sent from New York on the final voyage by first-class passenger Percy Seccombe.

Percy's father had been a Cunard captain and had sailed with Captain Turner of *Lusitania* on *Cephalonia*. Captain Turner had promised Percy's mother that he would look after him and his sister Elizabeth on the voyage. Percy's message reads:

Dear Mary,
I all most forgot to send you a line. Here is one, now take care of it, for it is valuable. Be good.
Piles of love.
P.

Neither Percy nor Elizabeth survived the sinking, but their remains were found. Percy was cremated and returned to his family in New Hampshire. Elizabeth was buried in Clonmel Cemetery in Mass Grave B on 14 May. A number of requests were received by local authorities from the Seccombe family, asking that Elizabeth be disinterred and sent home. Each time the request was refused on the grounds of public health.

An unusual elevated view of *Lusitania* taken while she was docked at Pier 54 in New York. It was from this same pier that she would sail on her final voyage and to which the Cunard liner *Carpathia* arrived with the survivors of *Titanic*. The image was taken during her last few years of service, as evidenced by the increased number of lifeboats that were added after the *Titanic* disaster. The pier shed was demolished in 1991 despite the efforts of preservationists to save it, although the pier itself remains.

Lusitania remained in New York for nine days and was opened to the public for a small fee. All proceeds from this were given to local charities. When her stay in New York was complete, she sailed back to Liverpool on 21 September. Once again she did not take the Blue Riband, but Vernon Brown, Cunard's American agent, stated: 'she's got something up her sleeve yet.'

Shown here docked in New York after her triumphal second voyage from Liverpool, *Lusitania* had just broken all existing transatlantic records and had become the first ship in history to cross the Atlantic in under five days. The passage had taken four days, nineteen hours and fifty-two minutes, and the average speed was 24.002 knots. She then settled into a regular routine. As time went on, her speed crept up; soon she was regularly breaking her own (as well as her sister's) records.

Another image of *Lusitania* docked at Pier 54 after her record-breaking crossing to New York. To celebrate the return of the Blue Riband to Britain, passengers and many of the ship's officers assembled in the first-class Dining Room on the final night of the voyage. The passenger who presided over the historic gathering stated:

> Although we applaud the *Deutschland* as a pacemaker, yet we cheered the *Lusitania* for beating her in the heroic struggle to wrest from the German giant the Blue Riband of the Atlantic. The line is again master of the ocean highway and this English victory is one in which the whole world joins us.

There was a 'guarantee period' of one year by the builders for any defects with the ship. During the summer of 1908, Cunard began submitting lists of claims to John Brown so that the cost of repair could be charged to the builder.

A HISTORY IN PICTURE POSTCARDS 69

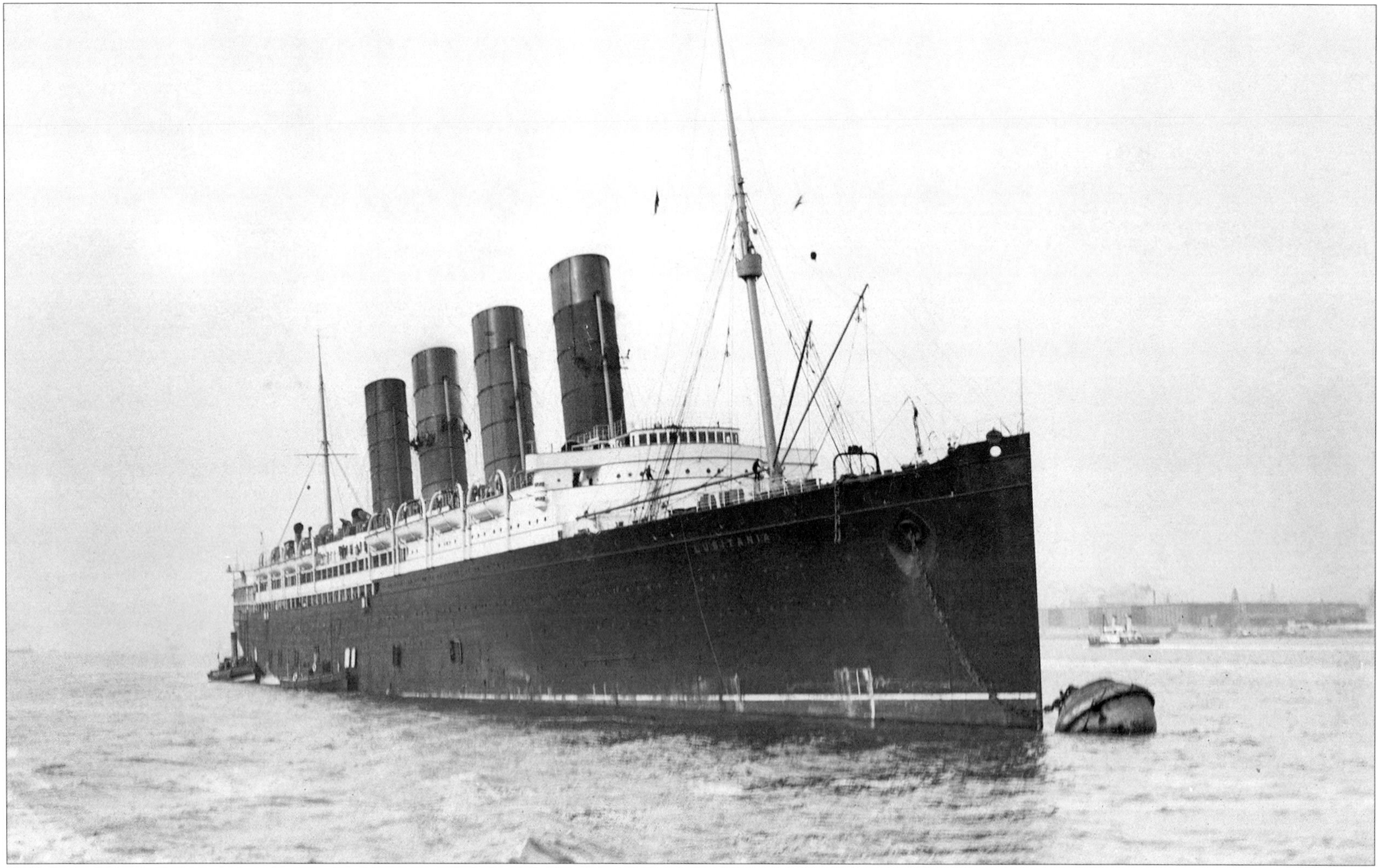

The general public at large had a difficult time telling many liners of the period apart, especially the two Cunard greyhounds. Someone has written across the top of this card 'R.M.S. *Mauritania* [sic] at Rock Ferry'. The ship pictured is, in fact, *Lusitania*. Even Captain Turner, who commanded *Lusitania* at various times, including on her final voyage, frequently misspelled the names of the two liners.

Opposite: Although the vibration had been greatly reduced after all the extra stiffening, Cunard was continually making small modifications to *Lusitania* to try to reduce it even further. One interesting fact discovered by Leonard Peskett, Cunard's naval architect, is that the amount of vibration changed depending on her draught. The higher the ship was riding in the water, the less vibration and noise there was.

Canvas dodgers are clearly visible covering the open areas of B and C decks. The dodgers were strung up shortly before coaling the vessel began because it was a very dirty affair. They were an attempt to keep coal dust from creeping into every nook and cranny of the vessel.

Also note the workmen on the second and third funnels applying a fresh coat of paint. This image dates from mid- to late 1909.

Lusitania at anchor in the Mersey.

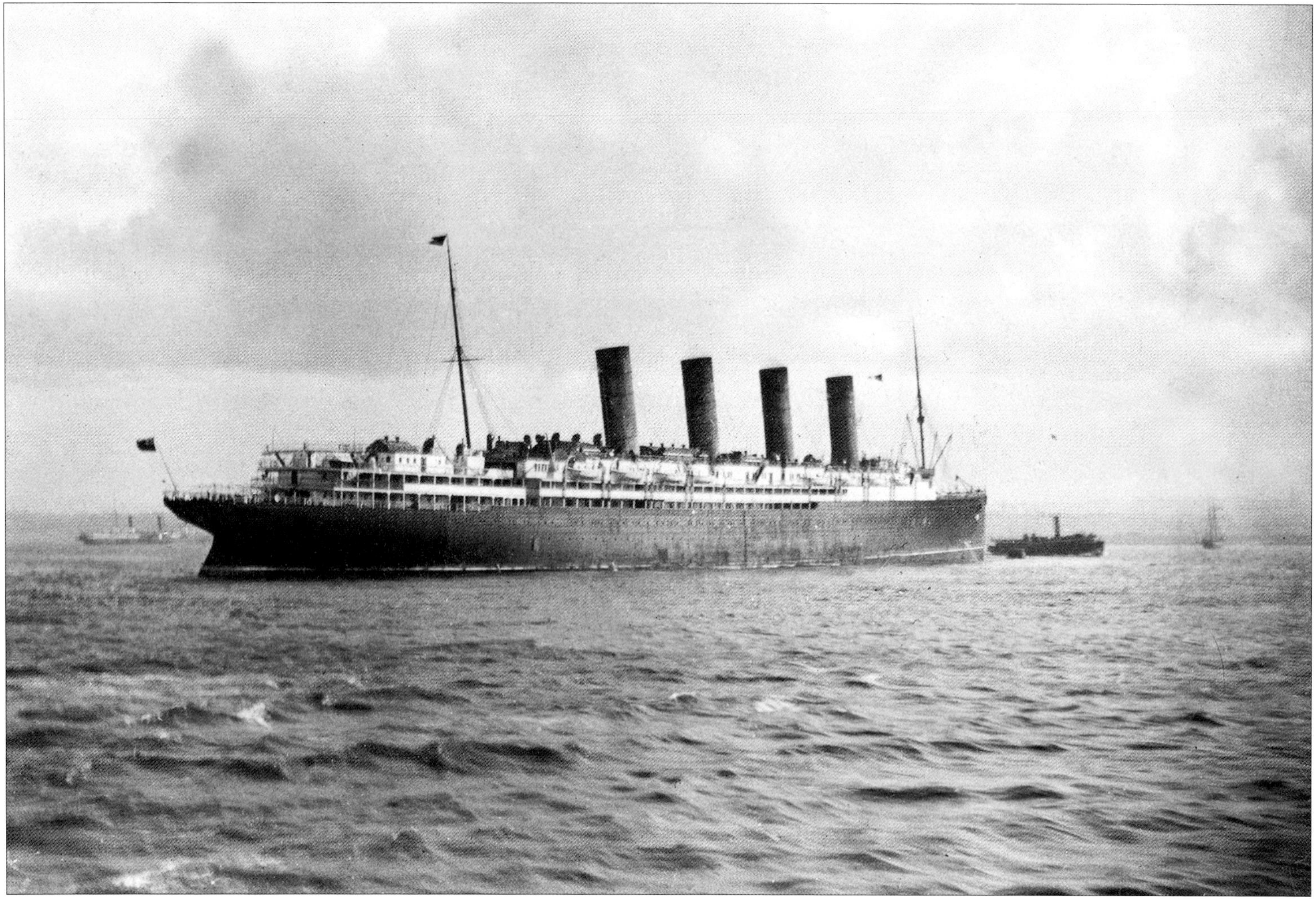

A HISTORY IN PICTURE POSTCARDS 75

A stunning view of *Lusitania* while docked at Pier 56 in New York. It must have been a fairly warm day because the majority of portholes are open, and a few have homemade 'wind scoops' to catch any hint of a breeze.

Lusitania and most other Cunard ships called Piers 53, 54, and 56 their home. These piers were located at the foot of West 14th Street. As in Liverpool, if the ship arrived after 8 p.m. passengers could stay on board for the night or disembark right away.

When a passenger booked a berth on a Cunard steamer, the booking was not guaranteed without a deposit of at least a quarter of the passage money or a minimum of $25 for each traveller. The balance of the fare had to be paid at least three weeks prior to departure.

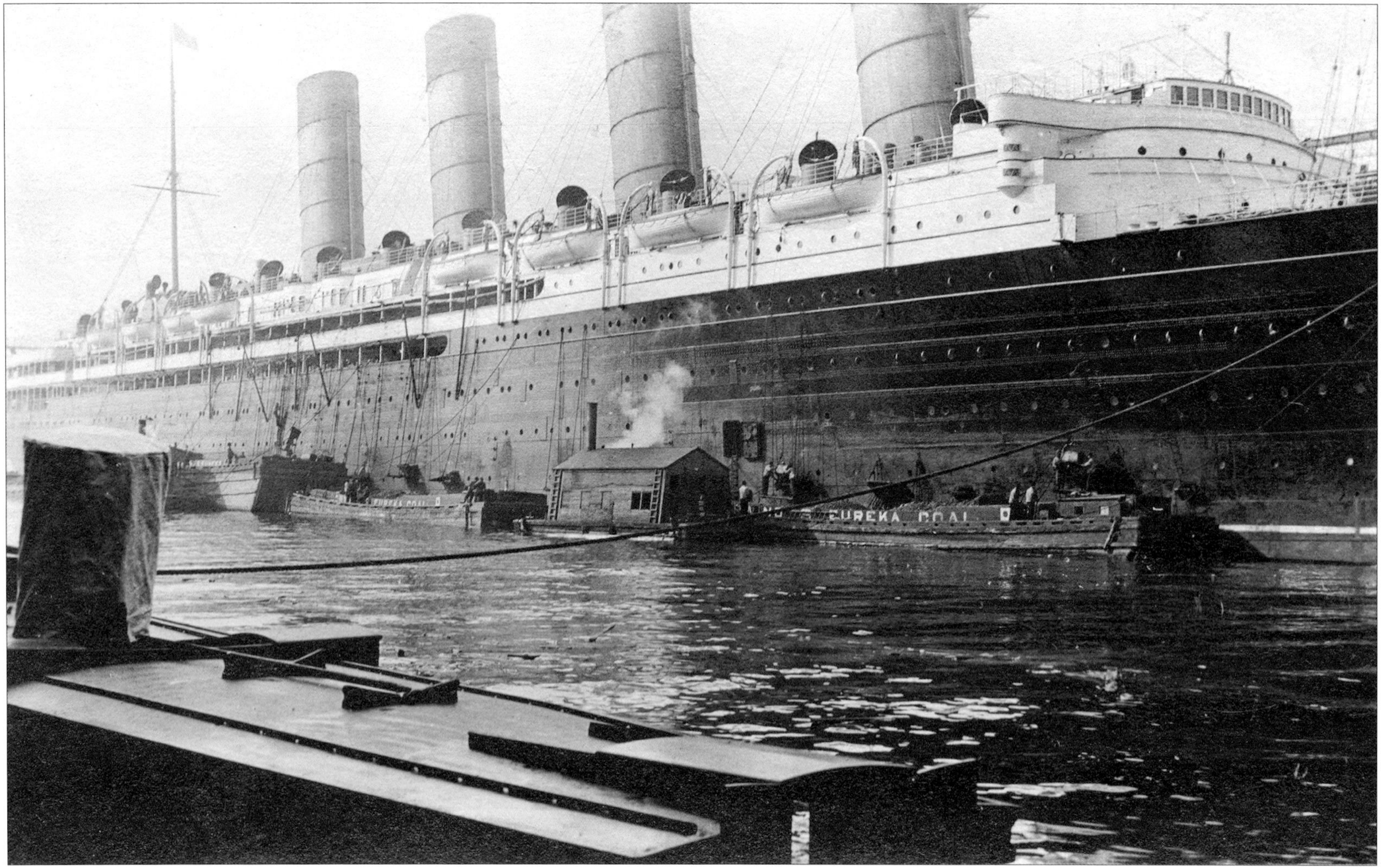
EUREKA COAL

Opposite: Among the amenities offered on most Cunard ships was an orchestra. During the voyage they played at different times and locations throughout the ship for the enjoyment of first- and second-class passengers. Those travelling third class generally had to provide their own entertainment.

At the time of *Lusitania*'s maiden voyage, the ship's orchestra would play at the following times and places, although, as the years passed, these hours were greatly extended:

    10 a.m. to 10.45 a.m. – Second-class Dining Room
    1 p.m. to 1.45 p.m. – First-class Dining Room
    3 p.m. to 4 p.m. – Second-class Dining Room or
       the saloon on Promenade Deck
    7.20 p.m. to 8.20 p.m. – First-class Dining Room
    9 p.m. to 10 p.m. – First-class drawing room or
       on Promenade Deck

Deckchairs and steamer rugs could also be rented from the deck steward for a minimal charge of 4s or $1 each. Each steamer rug came in its own sealed cardboard box with a special serial number so that passengers could identify their blanket. A note was printed in the passenger list for each voyage that assured the passengers that all the rugs, once they had been used, were sent to Cunard's cleaning facility and 'thoroughly cleaned before being reissued'.

Despite the fact that Liverpool was the home port for *Lusitania* and *Mauretania*, it was a rare occurrence when the Cunard sisters appeared there at the same time.

LIVERPOOL. R.M.S. Lusitania and Mauretania in Sandon Half Tide Dock.

LUSITANIA IN DOCK. W+CO

A very rare privately published card of *Lusitania* in the Huskisson Dock.

A prophetic photograph. In one of the finest photographs taken of *Lusitania*, she is steaming off the Old Head of Kinsale, very close to where she was torpedoed a few years later.

In this photograph, taken just a few moments after the previous image, *Lusitania* charges through the Irish Sea on her way to New York.

25 August 1913. Calm seas and fair weather prevail on the first day of *Lusitania*'s first crossing to New York after her turbine problems of December 1912. *Lusitania* and *Mauretania* were designed to be converted quickly into armed cruisers if the need arose, and each would sport twelve 6in guns. In the centre of the photograph is one of the slightly elevated rings that would have held a gun.

Aug 25- 1913 "Lusitania" Liverpool to N.Y.

Taken on the starboard side of Top of House, which was the highest passenger deck. The large skylight housing on the left is above the first-class Lounge, and the riveted 'wall' behind the passenger is the base of the No. 3 funnel.

Opposite: A second image taken during the same August 1913 crossing. This fascinating view looks aft on the port side of Top of House. In the foreground is one of *Lusitania*'s original 'clam-shell' ventilators. Unfortunately, these did not hold up to the rigours of service as expected. When the ventilator covers failed and needed replacing, they were substituted with cowl vents identical to those on *Mauretania*. The round mouth of one of these replacement vents can be seen immediately behind the clam-shell vent.

Also, if one looks carefully at the bottom of the vent in the foreground, the ship's camber can clearly be seen. Camber is the athwartships curvature of the deck that allowed for easier drainage of water to the side of the ship. On *Lusitania*, which was often referred to as a 'wet' ship, the camber was 18in, meaning the centre line of the deck was that much higher than the outboard edges.

Candid postcards of crew are quite rare. These two images were both taken while *Lusitania* was docked at Pier 56 in New York, and they both date to after the *Titanic* disaster because the extra lifeboats that were installed on the second-class deck house can be seen.

After the loss of *Titanic* in April 1912, steamship lines were required to put additional lifeboats on each ship of their fleet to ensure that every soul on board had a seat. Until the time of *Lusitania*'s loss, Cunard was forced to continuously alter the arrangement as the requirements changed year to year.

In a Cunard shareholders' report from shortly before the First World War, the company reported that in the two and a half years since *Titanic* had sunk they had spent over £76,700 'in order to comply with the varying government regulations in force from time to time. Under the new life-saving regulations as approved by the International Convention a large part of this expenditure will prove to have been a pure waste of money.'

Lusitania Life Boat

Taken on *Lusitania*'s final completed voyage to New York, this card shows one of her final boat drills. From available evidence, the officer standing on the rail in the white-topped hat is almost certainly First Officer Arthur Rowland Jones. Jones survived the sinking and was later lost at sea on 2 February 1918 while in command of HMT *Avanti*. He was only 38 years old.

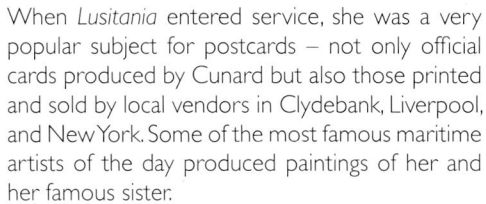

Have not heard of a situation in England yet hope to get something when I land.

When *Lusitania* entered service, she was a very popular subject for postcards – not only official cards produced by Cunard but also those printed and sold by local vendors in Clydebank, Liverpool, and New York. Some of the most famous maritime artists of the day produced paintings of her and her famous sister.

A HISTORY IN PICTURE POSTCARDS

Cunard R. M. S. „Lusitania".

Interiors

Left: The first-class Dining Room was a lofty apartment decorated in the style of Louis XVI with white-painted panelling and 'gilded enrichments'. The elliptical dome soared 30ft overhead and contained four paintings in the style of François Boucher, the eighteenth-century French painter. The room was designed to hold over 550 first-class passengers at a single sitting.

Although much of the overhead decoration throughout the ship appeared to be plaster, in many cases, such as the dome in the Dining Room, it was carved wood. Despite its greater initial expense over plaster, Cunard felt that carved wood would have lower maintenance costs over time.

At the beginning of the ship's career, long, dormitory-style tables dominated the lower level of the room, with smaller tables for five or six dotted throughout. As time went on, however, the long tables on the lower level were replaced with smaller ones. On the upper level, smaller tables had been installed originally, which gave this level a more intimate feel. In fact, in the early design stages Cunard considered using the upper level of the room as an exclusive à la carte restaurant but later rejected the idea.

Opposite: From a passenger list dated 17 April 1915 (*Lusitania*'s final completed voyage to New York), the mealtimes for first class are given as follows:

    Meals will be served in the Saloon at the following times.
    Breakfast from 8.30 to 10.; Luncheon at 1 p.m.; Dinner from 7 o'clock.
    The Bar will be closed at 11.30 p.m.

Church of England worship services were held in each class's respective Dining Room on Sunday mornings. The worship in first class was usually presided over by the captain or staff captain unless there was a travelling clergyman on board who asked to lead the service.

The Grand Dining Saloon. R.M.S. "LUSITANIA". 32,500 Tons. 790 ft. long. 88 ft. broad.

A HISTORY IN PICTURE POSTCARDS

First Class Lounge. R.M.S. "LUSITANIA". 32,500 Tons. 790 ft. long. 88 ft. broad.

The first-class Lounge was one of the largest rooms at sea. Decorated in the late Georgian style with soothing mahogany panelling and satinwood furniture, this apartment was the social hub of the ship.

According to Walter Gilbert of the Bromsgrove Guild, the group that designed much of the plasterwork throughout the liner, the theme in the Lounge was 'the Music of the Sea and of the Wind'. The twelve panels of the skylight depicted 'the playful tricks of the Amorini upsetting the emblems of time, represented by the signs of the Zodiac …'. Each panel represented a month of the year, the name of each month being in a different language.

FIRST CLASS LOUNGE. R.M.S LUSITANIA.

In an effort to make the rooms on board look as large as possible, the photographs that were to be used for postcards were taken from specific angles. What makes this postcard unique is the presence of people. This view looks aft.

When *Lusitania* sank, her hull cracked directly through the Lounge and the Dining Room below. Almost nothing identifiable is left of this room on the wreck.

On British liners, the Smoking Rooms were male preserves, places for after-dinner drinks and cigars while the ladies retired to the Lounges. German liners were quite the opposite, and women were encouraged to join their husbands after dinner. When *Lusitania* was being designed, Cunard reached out to the senior officers of each department and asked for their input on how the new liner could be improved. One suggestion, in fact, was to have a 'German-style' Smoking Room where men and women could meet after dinner.

James Miller, the consulting architect for much of *Lusitania*'s interiors, submitted a design for this room to Cunard in August 1906, but it was rejected by the company as not 'sufficiently attractive for the Smoke Room of this ship'. Miller reworked the plans and gave the room a more masculine feel. He resubmitted them to Cunard, which was quite pleased with the new rendering and accepted it.

The fireplace in the Smoking Room was the only functional one on board; the other fireplaces were only decorative. The smoke from this fireplace vented through the fourth funnel.

First Class Smoking Room. R. M. S. LUSITANIA.

Opposite: It was the social convention of the day to write notes or postcards home to loved ones as the ship was sailing. Steamship companies gave postcards and sheets of writing paper out by the thousands as free advertising. Some menus used on board even had detachable postcards at the top with views of various public rooms or ships of the Cunard fleet. For passengers departing from New York, a *Lusitania* passenger list states: 'Passengers desiring to have letters and telegrams forwarded by the pilot from Sandyhook must hand the same (fully prepaid) to the Purser within one hour after leaving the pier.'

All that remains of the first-class Library on the wreck are small sections of superstructure that formed the bays, with the windows still embedded in them.

FIRST CLASS LIBRARY, R.M.S. LUSITANIA.

This is the only known postcard of a second-class public room on board *Lusitania*. Although it is listed as the Smoking Room, it is in fact looking to starboard in the second-class Lounge on Boat Deck. In an effort to combat the vibration in the stern of the liner, this was one of the most heavily modified public rooms on board. On the left of the card can be seen the massive structural arches installed to ease the vibration.

Sinking and Aftermath

Built at the Kaiserlicher Werft in Danzig, Unterseeboot 20 (U-20) was ordered on 25 November 1910 and launched on 18 December 1912. She was commissioned on 5 August 1913 and was one of four vessels of this submarine class, carrying a thirty-five-member crew, including four officers.

She had a lucky career until 4 November 1916 when, under the command of Kapitänleutnant Walther Schwieger, of Lusitania fame, U-20 ran aground near Harbøøre, Denmark. After several unsuccessful attempts to refloat her, Schwieger ordered the crew to detonate torpedoes in her tubes to keep her from falling into British hands.

Over the years, there were several salvage expeditions to the wreck, and a number of important items were recovered. Many of these are now in Strandingsmuseum St George in Thorsminde, Denmark, including the conning tower, the deck gun, and a propeller.

Opposite: New York, 1 May 1915. *Lusitania* was scheduled to sail at 10 a.m. for her 202nd crossing, with passengers expecting to arrive in Liverpool on the following Saturday, 8 May. Earlier that morning, however, the British Admiralty had requisitioned RMS *Cameronia* for war service with the result that her passengers had to be transferred at the last minute to *Lusitania*, delaying the sailing until 12.30 p.m. On both sides of the Atlantic, even though there was much talk of a submarine attack, the number of bookings for this crossing was the highest since the war began.

When the all-clear signal had been given to indicate that there was no shipping in the river, Captain Turner ordered slow astern and backed out of the pier. High above on the catwalk on the roof of Pier 54, a lone cameraman filmed the departure. Once *Lusitania* was heading downriver, the order was given to increase speed and the liner made her way towards the open sea. Just outside New York Harbor, *Lusitania* met the Cunard liner *Caronia*, which had been requisitioned by the British government and was being used as an armed cruiser. After they had exchanged signals and messages, *Lusitania* slowly picked up speed for her voyage home.

Sinking of the Lusitania

Along the Irish Coast

1.

Sinking of the Lusitania
LUSITANIA
LIVERPOOL
Sighting the Submarine
2.

Sinking of the Lusitania

The explosion 3.

At about 1.20 p.m. at a distance of about 13 miles, U-20 spotted what was described in the logbook as a 'large passenger steamer' on the horizon. Immediately submerging and travelling at its maximum underwater speed of 9 knots, Schwieger hoped to be able to put U-20 into position for a clean shot. As the minutes passed, however, it seemed unlikely that he would be able to take a shot as the fast-moving liner was steaming away from the submarine towards the Irish coast. Suddenly, at about 1.40 p.m., Captain Turner ordered a turn to starboard, which would put *Lusitania* directly in front of U-20 and make an attack possible.

At 2.10 p.m., Schwieger ordered a single torpedo to be fired from a distance of about 700m. About a minute later, the torpedo struck the vessel somewhere below the bridge, and *Lusitania* took an immediate list to starboard. Her fate, as well as the fate of the 2,000 aboard, was sealed.

Opposite: On the morning of 30 April – the day before *Lusitania* left New York – the German submarine U-20, under the command of Kapitänleutnant Walther Schwieger, sailed from Emden, Germany. Her patrol route would take her up past the northern coast of Scotland and around the west and south coasts of Ireland. In the week before U-20 encountered *Lusitania* she had sunk several ships, including the Harrison liners *Candidate* and *Centurion*.

By the morning of Friday, 7 May, *Lusitania* had reached the south coast of Ireland, and passengers felt some relief at seeing land and knowing that they would disembark in Liverpool the following morning. After a bit of patchy fog that morning, most passengers were finishing luncheon or strolling on deck. Some were in their cabins preparing for disembarkation the following morning, little realising how their lives would shortly change forever.

Eighteen minutes after the torpedo struck, it was all over. One of the greatest ships the world had ever seen was now lying on her starboard side at the bottom of the cold Atlantic, and the lives of 2,000 innocent people had changed forever. Walther Schwieger and U-20 headed back out to sea and set a course for Germany.

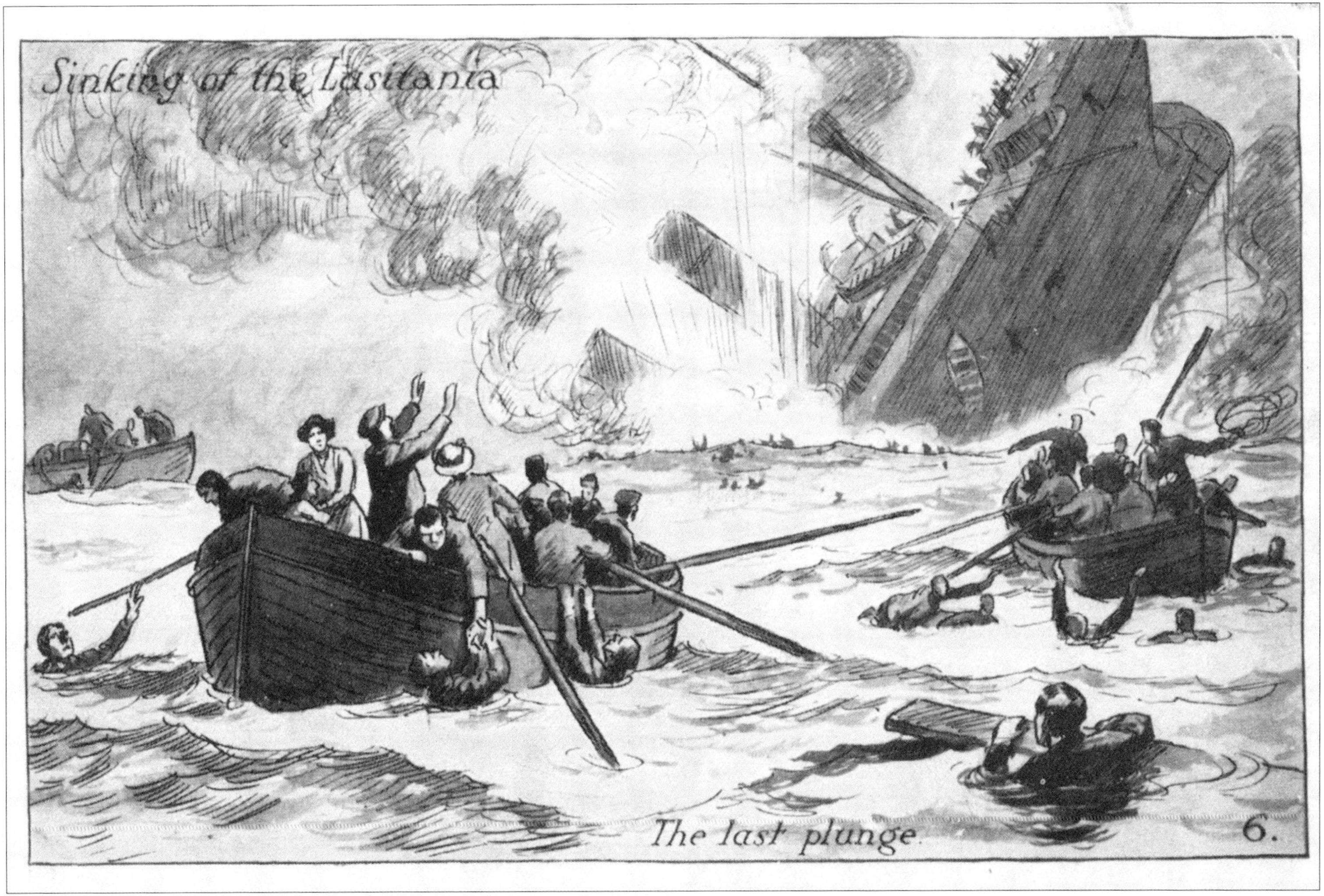
Sinking of the Lusitania
The last plunge
6.

Sinking of the Lusitania

Rescue Ships arrive 5.

By the evening of 7 May, just a few hours after *Lusitania* foundered, the first rescue ships arrived in Queenstown with both the living and the dead. Over the following few days, more and more boats that had gone to search for victims arrived with their grisly harvest. As the bodies arrived, they were laid out in the temporary morgues for those lucky enough to have survived to identify.

On Sunday, 9 May, 100 soldiers began digging the three mass graves in Clonmel Cemetery, about a mile outside Queenstown, to hold the hundreds of victims recovered and not returned home.

The first burials took place the following day with the Royal Garrison Artillery supplying parties of soldiers to load the coffins onto carts, which were then transported to the cemetery. They were met at the cemetery gate by sixty men of the 4th Irish Regiment, who carried them to the graves, and by a further 100 men of the same regiment who carried out the interments.

Opposite: About 1,200 men, women, and children died that day, and just under 300 bodies were recovered. The rest were either entombed in the ship or were carried away by the current, never to be seen again.

The sinking sent the world into political upheaval, but a Cunard ledger notes the event matter-of-factly: 'Sunk at 2.33 pm. Torpedoed by German Submarine. 8 miles S. by W., Old Head Kinsale.'

The Bishop of Cloyne officiated at a requiem mass that was held in Queenstown on Monday, 10 May. A Church of Ireland service was also conducted by the Reverend Archdeacon Daunt, and many survivors of the disaster attended both services.

The burials continued in both the mass graves and private graves until 16 June. The majority of bodies were buried with rapidity, and many were interred before they had been identified. As the months passed and their identities became known, family members requested that the remains of their loved ones be disinterred and forwarded for burial in their family plots. The reply from Cunard and the Burial and Sanitary Authorities was nearly always the same – that 'the removal would be detrimental to the public health', although early on some victims were exhumed and sent home at their family's expense.

As an incentive for fishermen and other locals who owned boats to recover the remains of victims, Cunard offered a reward of £1 for every body retrieved, and the American government added a further £1 for the body of each American found. The highest reward, however, would have belonged to the searcher who found millionaire Alfred Vanderbilt. His family offered a reward of £200. Unfortunately, his remains and those of hundreds of others were never located.

Once brought ashore, each recovered body was assigned a number, and the valuables found on it were sent to the Cunard office in Liverpool. Each body was also meant to be photographed, but this did not always happen. Cunard explained in an internal memo: '… all … bodies were supposed to have been photographed. As already explained, however, our photographer did not display much brilliancy, and it is quite possible that a body or two may have escaped his notice.'

Each casket also had the assigned body number chalked on it in the event that it needed to be located. Because of the confusion and the great haste with which the bodies were buried, there were a few that went missing. In a Cunard memo from 9 July, the company admitted that several bodies could not be found and that they had almost certainly been buried in Mass Grave C.

A Mr D. Morris wrote to Cunard asking if he could keep the lifebelt found on an unidentified victim, known only as 'Barry #2'. 'All the clothing found on the body, consisting of shirt, trousers, pants, socks and boots, have been destroyed, with the exception of a "crew" lifebelt which is now at this office, and which I would like to retain if no objection is raised.' Cunard replied that it had no objection to Mr Morris retaining the lifejacket.

This sign was the first marker placed on the graves to indicate their location. It was re-lettered every few years and was eventually removed. In 1986 a fundraising drive was begun to finally erect the first official headstones at each of the mass graves. For decades, local caretakers had tended the graves, but by the late 1950s, they had become run-down. The Cunard office in Queenstown wrote to the general manager in Liverpool, advising him that 'some improvement should be made' to the condition of the graves. An estimate was received, and the beds of the graves were refreshed with new plantings.

Opposite: When the United States entered the war, one of the most 'popular' pilgrimage spots for American servicemen was the graveyard outside of Queenstown. They usually had a photograph taken with the sign.

On the first anniversary of the sinking, the Queenstown Urban District Council organised 'Decoration Day'. The commemoration took place at 3.30 p.m. on Sunday, 7 May 1916. On that same day, flags on all Cunard ships and buildings around the world flew at half mast to honour those lost in the sinking.

LUSITANIA GRAVES.
BY ORDER OF THE CUNARD STEAMSHIP CO LTD.
M. SAUNDERS & SONS.

SACRED
TO THE MEMORY OF
FRANCIS WILLIAM LANCASTER
4TH SON OF
WILLIAM LOCKE LANCASTER
WHO LOST HIS LIFE IN THE
"LUSITANIA" DISASTER
7. MAY 1915, AGED 48 YEARS.

ALFRED SCOTT WITHERBEE JR.
BORN
JUNE 27TH 1911.
DIED MAY 7TH 1915.
A VICTIM OF THE "LUSITANIA"
FOULLY MURDERED BY
GERMANY.

When news of the sinking became known, riots broke out all over the UK against anyone with a German-sounding name. This view shows the aftermath of a riot in Liverpool, *Lusitania*'s home port. The message on the back of the card reads: 'Results of Raid following the Sinking of the *Lusitania*, Liverpool, England.'

Opposite, left: Second-class passenger Francis Lancaster was lost in the sinking. When his remains were recovered, he was assigned #12 and buried in Clonmel Cemetery on 10 May in Mass Grave A; **right:** A postcard of the grave of body #243. Positively identifying those lost proved to be a difficult task in many cases. Although the grave is marked as that of three-year-old Alfred Scott Witherbee, there was some question at the time about whether the body found was actually his. Mrs Witherbee, who lost both her child and her mother in the sinking, had claimed body #243 as her son. Arthur Luck, however, who had lost his wife and both sons in the sinking, thought body #243 was his young son Kenneth. After a brief tug-of-war over the body, the Witherbee family triumphed and buried the boy as Alfred even though the description of the remains was a closer match to Kenneth Luck.

This lifeboat (#A2, the forwardmost collapsible on the port side) was recovered a few days after the disaster. It had overturned, and several bodies were found beneath it. It became a powerful propaganda tool and for several years was displayed around the UK at various fundraising events for the war effort. It is almost certainly the boat mentioned in this Cunard memo: 'Referring cable from New York boat was capsized when floated into Schull and bodies of four women and three children were found underneath and in the vicinity …'.

The boat was eventually donated to the Broadstairs Town Council and was on display there for at least thirty years. Its present whereabouts is unknown. The sign above it reads:

> *Lusitania* Raft. This raft is one from the S.S. *Lusitania* torpedoed by a German submarine off the coast of Ireland May 7th 1915, [it] was washed ashore having several bodies aboard. Presented to the town council June 7th 1917. Lest We Forget.

LUSITANIA RAFT, BROADSTAIRS

Propaganda

The *Lusitania* graves in Queenstown became a focal point for British propaganda. On this card, a photograph of the three mass graves was paired with the first German *Lusitania* medal produced by Karl Goetz. According to a letter written by Goetz many years later, the original intent of the medal was the 'censure of the Cunard Line for gross neglect. Only this my medal wanted to show … for myself the *Lusitania* case was not an event for triumph …'.

On the original issue of the medal, the date of the sinking was listed as 5 Mai [May] 1915. This honest mistake on Goetz's part was used by the British government to claim that Germany had intended all along to sink the liner and had produced this medal beforehand to commemorate the event. The incorrect date was, according to Goetz himself, 'a writing error on my part. I took this date out of a newspaper account and corrected it later to the 7th of May. The piece itself was cast for the first time in August [19]15.'

Around 300,000 copies were issued by the British government as propaganda pieces. In fact, this medal was so successful in stirring up anti-German sentiment that the War Office of the Kingdom of Bavaria issued a decree stating that 'the further manufacture and sale of the *Lusitania* medal … is … forbidden'.

A MEMORIAL TO GERMAN SAVAGERY
The three large graves at Queenstown where the bodies of 178 of the "Lusitania" victims rest.
(Inset is the medal which was struck in Germany to celebrate this dastardly crime.)
Printed in England

Opposite: Despite the incredible tragedy, the loss of so many children aboard *Lusitania* was a huge boon to the British propaganda machine. The artist Louis Raemaeker was one of the best-known and most prolific propaganda artists of the First World War.

LES PETITES VICTIMES
DE LA LUSITANIA.

THE LITTLE VICTIMS
OF THE LUSITANIA.

APRÈS LA LUSITANIA.

LE CAUCHEMAR D'HÉRODE.

HAROD'S NIGHTMARE.

— Maman ! maman ! pourquoi ?

Salon de la Guerre – L. BOUCHER – AUX VICTIMES DU LUSITANIA – TO THE VICTIMS OF THE "LUSITANIA" – ЖЕРТВАМЪ ЛЮЗИТАНІИ.

After producing his first *Lusitania* medal, Goetz's reason for producing it was twisted so far away from what he had intended by the British propaganda machine that he produced a far less well-known *Lusitania* medal, shown here, in an attempt to undo some of the damage his first medal had caused. An interesting aspect of this medal is that Goetz himself is seen on the obverse as the bearded artist holding the sketchbook.

"LUSITANIA"-PROPAGANDA. By K. GOETZ.

Obverse:—Mr. A. J. Balfour making a speech, holding Goetz's "Lusitania" medal in his hand; around, "It is difficult to refrain from satire"; below, "The 'Lusitania' medal gives Lord Balfour something to make a speech about, 9.xi.1916." *Reverse:*—"English propaganda-work in Sweden." A Highlander playing bagpipes and holding a placard, "English Pamphlet: A German Sea-Victory, 1916," with reproduction of the medal.

BRITISH MUSEUM. Printed at the Oxford University Press.

Even three years after the sinking, *Lusitania* was still a powerful propaganda tool. The Lord Rhondda mentioned on the placard in front of the tank is David Alfred Thomas. Both he and his daughter, Margaret Mackworth, survived the sinking. Lord Rhondda died on 3 July 1918, about two months after this photograph was taken.

R.M.S. "LUSITANIA" CUNARD LINE BOUND FROM NEW YORK TO LIVERPOOL, WAS TORPEDOED OFF QUEENSTOWN BY A GERMAN SUBMARINE, WITH A LOSS OF 1,500 LIVES, MAY 7TH, 1915.

Two early images of *Lusitania* – one of her during her trials and one as she lay in the Mersey – turned into propaganda cards.

Cunard Liner, "Lusitania," *(Turbine).*

Torpedoed and Sunk by German Submarine off the Old Head of Kinsale, on the South Coast of Ireland, on 7th May, 1915.

32,000 Tons; 68,000 H.P.; Speed, 26½ knots; Length 787 ft. Breadth, 88 ft.; Depth, 60 ft.

128 RMS LUSITANIA